MAGIC

A
Strange Science
B O O K

Sylvia Funston

Illustrations by Joe Weissmann

Owl Books are published by **Maple Tree Press Inc.**
51 Front Street East, Suite 200, Toronto, Ontario M5E 1B3

The Owl colophon is a trademark of Bayard Canada.
Maple Tree Press Inc. is a licensed user of trademarks of Bayard Canada.

Distributed in the United States by Firefly Books (U.S.) Inc.
230 Fifth Avenue, Suite 1607, New York, NY 10001

We acknowledge the financial support of the Canada Council for the Arts, the Ontario
Arts Council, and the Government of Canada through the Book Publishing Industry
Development Program (BPIDP) for our publishing activities.

Dedication
For Ben and Olly

Cataloguing in Publication Data
Funston, Sylvia
        Magic

"A strange science book".
Includes index.
ISBN 1-894379-33-0 (bound).—ISBN 1-894379-34-9 (pbk.)

1. Magic—Juvenile literature. 2. Science and magic—Juvenile literature.
I. Weissmann, Joe, 1947- II. Title.

GV1548.F85 2003   j133.4'3   C2002-900410-1

Design & art direction: Word & Image Studio Inc. (www.wordandimagedesign.com)
Illustrations: Joe Weissmann

Photo Credits
Page 6: Raymond Gehman/CORBIS/MAGMA; 8: Jim Zintgraff/The Rock Art Foundation;
10: Roger Ressmeyer/CORBIS/MAGMA; 12: Lindsay Hebberd/CORBIS/MAGMA;
13: Michael Freeman/CORBIS/MAGMA; 17: Corinium Museum, Cirencester; 20: Japack
Company/CORBIS/MAGMA; 21: Cindy Kassab/CORBIS/MAGMA; 23: Papilio/CORBIS/
MAGMA; 24: Caroline Penn/CORBIS/MAGMA; 25: Stephen Frink/CORBIS/MAGMA;
28: Farrell Grehan/CORBIS/MAGMA; 29: John Clegg/ARDEA; 33: Buddy Mays/CORBIS/
MAGMA; 34: Kobal Collection; 37: Dave Sandford/Hockey Hall of Fame

Printed in Hong Kong

A   B   C   D   E   F

Contents

Do You Believe in MAGIC?

If you could enroll at Hogwarts School of Witchcraft and Wizardry, you would have to cram your head full of all sorts of weird and wonderful facts. One of the first really practical things you would learn is the difference between magic and "magick."

The magician who entertains by pulling rabbits out of a hat or making things disappear is a master of illusion based on tricks—you'll find more on this type of magic later in the book. The other kind of magician claims to change events by using rituals, spells, magic tools or words to tap into a mystical force of nature. He or she is no entertainer, but is practicing the ancient and serious art of magick. And that's what this book is mostly about.

In the pages that follow, you'll discover how magic can be intended for both good and harm, why magicians were the world's first doctors and scientists, and how some ancient ideas about the workings of magic have echoes in modern science. You'll find out why words became magical, and the truth behind fortune-telling, magical healing, superstitions, and zombies. Join in the search for the philosopher's stone, which is supposed to change lead into gold and help the lucky magician who owns it live a very long time!

Do you believe in magic? Maybe this book can help you find out.

Magical
MYSTERIES

The Aurora Borealis, or Northern Lights, are seemingly magical waves of light that appear in the night sky. They are caused by high-energy particles from the solar wind, a stream of energy from the sun.

Start with a little "light" magic...

What Is Magic?

Imagine you live in a universe that's filled with an invisible cosmic spirit. This powerful force of nature flows constantly from the stars to the Earth, where highly trained people learn to channel it through precious gems, plants or other objects. Or they might tap into the power of the force through the careful use of special words and symbols. These are influential people whose words and deeds are taken very seriously.

Sounds like it could be science, doesn't it? But it isn't; the cosmic spirit is an explanation of where magic comes from, and those who claim to use it are magic-makers of all kinds. For thousands of years, people all over the world believed in ideas like this, and some still do. But even people who believe totally in magic have never understood what it was or how it worked.

In modern times, we have come to realize just how close to the truth the idea of the cosmic spirit might be. Our planet actually *is* bombarded by cosmic energy from the stars. The sun, our nearest star, sends out a constant stream of electrified gas we call the solar wind. When our planet's powerful magnetic force field slows down the solar wind, some of the high-energy particles in it can leak through the force field at the earth's magnetic poles. These particles strike the atmosphere and release energy that we see as moving curtains of colored light. We call this the Northern Lights. The energy given off by oxygen creates the greenish-yellow lights in the Northern Lights, while nitrogen creates the blue light.

Ride the Wind

The solar wind travels up to 800 kilometers (500 miles) per second, and we'd love to channel all that energy. One way would be to equip spacecraft with huge solar sails. In the future, astronauts might sail to Mars or Jupiter, pushed along by the magic of the solar wind.

Sound and Light Show

If you have dry, frizzy hair, wear glasses and have a pine tree you can lean against the next time the Northern Lights are in the sky, you might hear them as well as see them. How? Your hair and the needles of the pine tree vibrate to the very low frequency sounds given off by the lights. With luck, your ears will turn these vibrations into sound. Your glasses help boost the sound as they transfer the vibrations directly to the bones in your head.

Magical
MYSTERIES

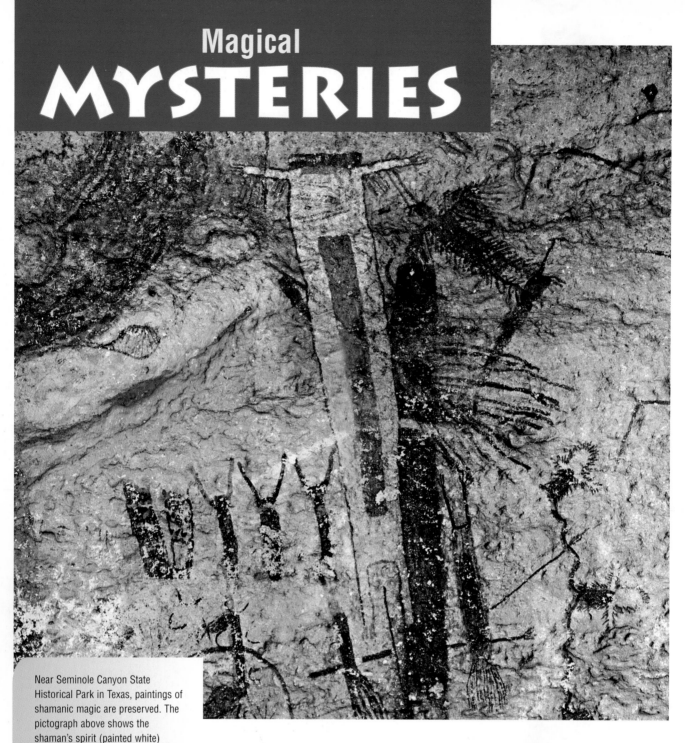

Near Seminole Canyon State Historical Park in Texas, paintings of shamanic magic are preserved. The pictograph above shows the shaman's spirit (painted white) leaving his physical body (painted black) to fight past the red monster and reach the spirit world. You can see the shaman's typical feathered wings and antler headdress.

Who Were the First Magicians?

The earliest magicians—as early as the prehistoric Stone Age—were most likely men and women who had special gifts. They were seen to be people who could take control of the magic that existed all around and use it to change things. Paintings on cave walls show magicians known as shamans who could slip into a trance, during which they made contact with the spirit world. These paintings, or pictographs, also show the people witnessing the shaman's trance, and the monsters that guard the barrier between the worlds.

Dream a Little Dream

In ancient Egypt, apprentice magicians had to undergo years of hard training. When they finally qualified, they set to work curing the sick. One of their treatments involved having their patients sleep in the temple. Upon waking, patients were encouraged to tell their dreams so that they could be interpreted. This early form of psychotherapy would have been helpful to patients suffering from stress or anxiety.

Wearing Many Hats

From healing the sick to bringing rain, from communicating with spirits to telling the future, magicians have traditionally worn many hats. And, depending where you lived, the magic man or woman—so important to the community—was known as magician, shaman, wizard, witch, soothsayer, sorceror, witchdoctor or necromancer.

In some places, people with sicknesses such as epilepsy or schizophrenia were seen as having special communication with the magic spirits that were invisible to everyone else. But magicians were often healers themselves, knowing how plants could cure people and offering good advice.

Throughout history, most natural forces were complete mysteries because no one had the science to explain them. But, really, magicians were the world's first scientists and doctors. To attempt to change things like the weather and people's health, magicians studied those unseen forces to see if they could be influenced by potions, spells and special ceremonies. If instead they had studied how the universe worked, maybe they would have come up with scientific theory.

JUST A JOB

A number of jobs were once closely associated with magic. Why do you think the people who practiced the following occupations were considered to be magic users? (Answers on page 40.)

| Doctors | Midwives | Blacksmiths |
| Barbers | Shepherds | Gravediggers |

Magical
MYSTERIES

If you're in the Northern Hemisphere, this is one of the first star groups you see. It is known as the Big Dipper, the Great Bear (Ursa major), the Plough or Charles's Wain (or wagon). What's magic about it? No matter how the constellations move, the two stars that form the right side of the dipper always point to the North Star.

Make a magical wish on a star.

How Does Magic Work?

If science is the study of the universe based on how things are connected, and how things influence other things, how is it different from magic? Unlike magicians, scientists have to show clear cause and effect. They have to prove that connections actually exist, and they do this through experimentation.

Magic relies on invisible and mysterious connections in the universe, things that have been believed since ancient times. Astrology—predicting human events by the movement of stars and planets—was a natural outcome of this way of thinking, and it has had magical connections for thousands of years. Magicians also studied the movements of the moon and the sun to predict planting and harvesting times. And they performed carefully scheduled ceremonies and rituals, or patterned ways of doing things, to make sure the spirit world remained happy and continued to bless them with sunshine, rain and food.

Magical Thinking

Can you remember ever being convinced that the moon was following you? According to Jean Piaget, a scientist who studied children's behavior, this magical view of the world, in which we think objects and events are under our control, is one of the stages we all go through as we grow up.

Magical thinking starts when we are just babies. A newborn can't tell the difference between itself, its parents or the world around it. And why should it? After all, few people ignore a crying baby, so food, dry clothes, toys or cuddles magically appear on demand.

When you were very young did you sometimes feel that objects had some sort of magical connection to you? A Swiss psychologist named Jean Piaget described how a young girl would never play with marbles that she'd won because she feared she'd lose them. The girl believed that those particular marbles were still connected to whoever lost them and would want to return to that person.

Trail of Bread Crumbs?

About 20 years ago, a scientist named Rupert Sheldrake asked himself why rats always seemed to solve a maze faster when other rats had solved it before them. Did the rats share their secrets over late night mugs of hot chocolate? Hardly. Yet what Sheldrake suggested was almost as fantastic. He thought that the learning done by the first rats to solve the maze might continue on as some kind of mysterious energy, to be picked up later by newcomers to the maze.

Magical MYSTERIES

Caught a cold? Go see a witchdoctor!

The people of India celebrate Holi, the Festival of Colors, with two rituals of imitative magic. Drenching each other with vibrant colors imitates and invites the colors of spring. To celebrate a story of the triumph of good, people build bonfires, like the fire that spared a devoted prince named Prahlad while consuming his evil sister Holika.

Types of Magic

How do the mysterious connections of magic work? Sometimes magic is imitative, and sometimes it's contagious. To make imitative magic work, you have to believe that things that are alike can influence each other. If you're a wizard and someone comes to you complaining of pains in the liver, you give them a potion made out of a plant with liver-shaped leaves. Today we know that plants have the ability to cure ailments because of the chemicals they contain, not because they look like the part of the body that has to be cured. But this "like curing like" idea can still be found in the alternative form of medicine called homeopathy. It treats disease by using tiny amounts of a drug that, in large quantities, produces symptoms like those of the disease it's intended to cure.

According to contagious magic, a lasting bond exists between things that were once connected. That's why fingernail clippings or locks of hair are used in love spells, or spells to harm a person, in the belief that anything the sorcerer does to them will affect the person they belonged to. As strange as that might sound, it is no stranger than the world of quantum physics, where scientists study what goes on in particles too tiny for ordinary microscopes to see. Events occur that could easily be mistaken for magic: things can be in two places at once, a current can flow in both directions at the same time and two particles that become separated can continue to act as though they're still connected.

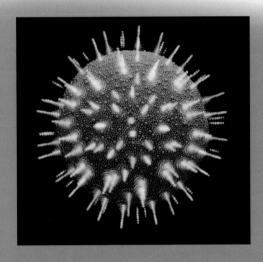

Like Curing Like

If vaccinations contain the viruses or bacteria that cause the disease you don't want to catch, how do they work? The viruses or bacteria in a vaccine are dead. When they're injected into you, the killer cells in your immune system have a chance to recognize their shapes. They can then develop a battle plan to kill any living viruses or bacteria that match these shapes if they come across them later on. Scientists have created a form of the AIDs-causing HIV virus, shown above, that carries a suicide gene. When this altered form of the virus meets infected immune cells, it forces them to commit suicide, preventing the virus from spreading. It's the first time HIV is being used to kill off HIV.

The Magic World of Tiny Particles

Everything around you is made up of tiny particles called atoms. They're so tiny, 10 million of them side by side would barely span the letter "o" in this word! Scientists dream about building machines that have parts just a few thousand atoms across. Something this small could cruise through your blood vessels to dispense medicine, or search out and destroy dust mites in your pillows and mattress.

MAGIC MAZE

Shamans use meditation as a sort of launching pad to take off on their spirit journeys. Some people use a colored geometric picture known as a mandala to focus their meditation—Tibetan mandalas were painstakingly made out of millions of grains of colored sand. In the Middle Ages, Europeans used mazes instead of mandalas to help them concentrate. Can you find your way from the magic number square at the entrance to the center of the maze? It may be easy when you trace the path with your finger, but can you do it using just your eyes?

The Magic ARTS

How well can you spell?

Magical Writing

More than 6,000 years ago, someone in China painted the Chinese numbers 5, 7 and 8 on some pottery. They're the earliest signs of written language yet discovered. Writing might have been around for a long time, but it wasn't until very modern times that most people could read. Before then, if you weren't royalty, a member of the ruling class, a priest, monk, scientist, doctor or magician, learning to read was out of the question.

When words are written down, they represent every idea we've ever had and make it possible for us to share knowledge. Knowledge is power, and anyone who can read has access to that power. Long ago, non-readers could only marvel at what they didn't understand and so they developed superstitious beliefs about written words. No wonder words became magical.

Magicians kept their knowledge secret by memorizing spells and rituals or writing them in code in spell books known as grimoires. But codes could be broken—until now. In the weird world of quantum physics, the act of measuring a quantum object alters it. So scientists use quantum objects—such as the photon particles found in faint pulses of light—to carry information. Tapping into an information-carrying pulse of light has the same effect as measuring some of its photons. It alters the information and alerts its owners that someone's trying to break their code.

Lucky Numbers

You might have grown up thinking that 7 is a magical number. But if you grew up in China and speak Mandarin, two of your luckiest numbers are 8 and 9. Why? In the Mandarin dialect, the number 8 is pronounced "ba," which is a variation of "fa," a word meaning to prosper. And the number 9 sounds exactly like "jiu," which means long-lasting. Many Mandarin-speaking people buy cell-phone numbers containing 8 or 9, and September 9, 1999, was a very popular day for weddings. In both China and Japan, 4 is the unluckiest number of all, since it is pronounced "shi," a word which also means death.

CREATE A MAGIC SQUARE

A magic square is made up of letters that spell the same words read up or down, from the left or from the right. They represent rare and powerful magic, as there are only seven originals from the ancient world: the one at right was found in Britain, and one was found in the ruins of Pompeii (a city in Italy destroyed by the eruption of volcanic Mount Vesuvius). At first a religious symbol (the word TENET, which means a religious belief, forms a cross in the center of the square), this square later became a protective magic charm. Can you find words to make your own magic square? Hint: it might be easier if you use words made up of three letters instead of five.

17

SECRET OF THE RUNES

Runes, meaning "secrets," are ancient Scandinavian symbols of magical power. They also were used as an alphabet. Vikings, the Norse raiders of the eighth to tenth centuries, engraved them on their swords to give them strength in battle or painted them on their houses as charms against evil. Magicians used them to cast spells and look into the future. Make your own set of runes by painting the symbols on small pebbles, or pieces of paper or cardboard. Magicians once used blood for the symbols, but magic marker will do!

Fehu
Prosperity will be yours.

Uruz
Invest energy in personal growth.

Thurisaz
Unhappiness before a new beginning.

Ansuz
An important message might arrive.

Raidho
A spiritual quest moves you closer to your goal.

Kenaz
You'll find your way through difficulties.

Gebo
Gifts of any sort, including friendship.

Wunjo
Expect changes for the better.

Reading the Runes

Put your runes into a box or a bag. Shut your eyes and pick out five, laying them out as shown to the right. Place the first rune in position 1, the second in position 2 and so on. Each position relates in a different way to your situation.

Rune 1 reveals your general situation.

Rune 2 shows what will happen if you change nothing in your situation.

Rune 3 identifies what will happen if you do make changes.

Rune 4 tells you which part of your situation is most open to change.

Rune 5 confirms what will remain constant in your situation.

2. *Ingwaz*

3. *Kenaz*

4. *Ehwo*

1. *Sowilo*   5. *Ofhalo*

Hagalaz

Joy comes after hardship.

Naudhiz

Recognize what you need to reach your goal.

Isa

Time to struggle free of present problem.

Jera

Give things time to happen naturally.

Iwaz

Success in the face of adversity.

Perthro

Sometimes you have to give in to fate.

Elhaz

You'll triumph and resist temptation.

Sowilo

You are set to achieve your most difficult goal.

Tiwaz

Courage and sacrifice will see justice done.

Berkano

Peace and health will be yours.

Ehwo

Co-operate to achieve your goal.

Mannaz

Use your intelligence, reason and memory.

Laguz

Listen to the messages in your dreams.

Ingwaz

Don't rush to solve a problem.

Dagaz

A surprise is on its way.

Ofhalo

Examine what you were taught by your elders.

Wyrd

Some things must remain forever a mystery.

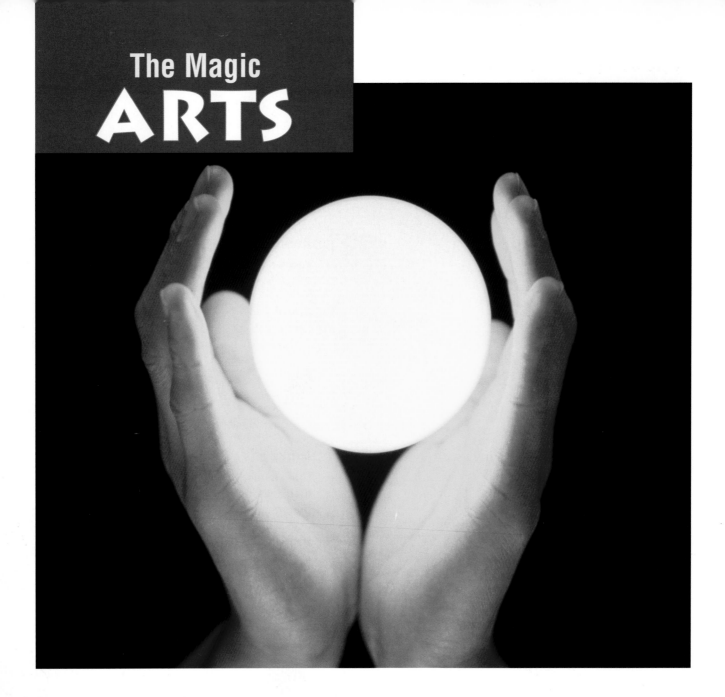

Seeing the Future

Any self-respecting magician has to be able to tell the future. Some have used astrology to advise people on the best time to go to war or get married. Some consult runes or read palms. Others prefer scrying—the art of seeing the future in a shiny surface. They can use a mirror or a sword blade, or even a pool of black ink. But the favorite scrying tool has always been a crystal ball.

It was once thought that scrying objects, such as crystal balls, work because they contain iron oxides, just like the human body does. This was supposed to make them magnetically attractive to psychic messages, which set up vibrations inside them. But how was the crystal-ball-gazer supposed to see these vibrations? In the vision section of their brains, humans were thought to store a

I see a long sea voyage...

magnetic force known as odyle, which supposedly streamed from a magician's eyes as he or she looked into the crystal ball. Vibrations from the crystal were then transmitted back into the brain of the gazer, creating visions in the stored odyle.

It's odd how old explanations often have a kernel of truth in them. Your brain might not contain magnetic odyle, but your body is mostly water, and the atoms that make up water contain spinning particles known as electrons. The tiny circular currents these electrons generate do create a seemingly magic magnetic field around your body.

IT'S ALL ABOUT YOU

Why do fortune-telling techniques always seem to give you a message that relates to your situation? Turn to page 40 for the answer.

All in Your Head

Most scientists agree that visions in a crystal ball occur because of the way your brain works, but not because of odyle. If you block out all outside distractions, turn down the lights and concentrate on staring for a long time into a crystal ball, your mind will slip into the kind of state it's in just before you fall asleep. Anything you see in the ball will be dream-like visions produced by your very imaginative subconscious mind.

Local Forecast

Shamans studied the moon to predict the best times to plant and harvest. Rainmakers performed ceremonies at certain times to bring on the rain. Is it possible they knew about the "air tides" that have been recently discovered? As the moon orbits the Earth, its gravitational force pulls water up towards it, and the traveling bulge of water creates high tides. The moon's pull can also lift the land and the earth's atmosphere. The air tides it creates might somehow be linked to the increased cloudiness and rainfall during certain phases of the moon.

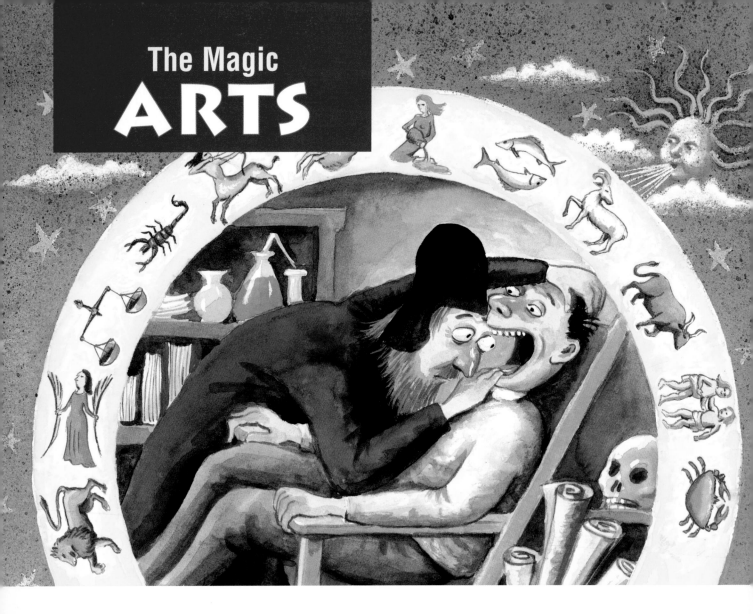

The Magic ARTS

Healing Magic

Touch two hanged men and call me in the morning.

If you were a surgeon a thousand years ago in medieval Europe, you'd probably have operated on a patient only when the right constellation was dominant in the sky. Back then it was believed that different signs of the zodiac governed different parts of the body. An English doctor's case notes show that he used astrology to help him make a diagnosis and often based his treatment on imitative magic. For instance, his preferred prescription for a swollen throat was to touch the hand of a man who'd been hanged!

Meanwhile, in North America and parts of Asia, it was thought that sickness or injury upset the sacred balance between spirits and humans. So a shaman would call upon all the spirits he, or sometimes she, could conjure up to help identify the cause of the trouble. Some shamans left the curing of the disease to a medicine man, who might suck out the disease spirits from the patient's body or use the healing touch of massage.

Mind-over-Magic

Scientists have discovered that patients boost the power of their immune system when they use self-hypnosis to picture killer cells in their blood attacking and destroying harmful viruses. Cancer patients who imagine their killer cells are white sharks swimming through their blood vessels and gobbling up cancer cells have achieved similar results.

Magic Mistletoe

You might have seen mistletoe, shown above, used as a decoration during the winter holidays. But more than 2,000 years ago ancient Celts believed that this plant's magic power could frighten away evil spirits. Today's researchers are hoping this is true. They are working to find a way to bind mistletoe's poison to a patient's infection-killing cells. The hope is that when these doctored cells attack cancer cells or cells that are infected with HIV, they'll deliver a poisonous punch that will knock out diseased cells without harming healthy ones.

Some people recover from illness without any kind of treatment. So the doctor or shaman who used magic to treat an illness was bound to be successful some of the time. But they might have achieved even greater success than this. The mind-body connection is very strong and the mind can often help heal the body if it is totally convinced that a certain ritual, magic spell, healing touch or prescription will bring about a cure. If the patients believed in the power of the magic, it might have helped them to feel better.

The Magic ARTS

Voodoo dolls and fetishes like these are supposed to give a sorceror power over his or her enemies. Need some magic fast? Just go to a fetish market.

Scary Magic

Magic can be used for good or for harm. But ask an expert on magic, and you will be told that bringing the dead back to life is always a bad idea, no matter how good your intentions might be. Necromancers were known for making the dead appear to rise up from the grave by placing a special ring on a finger or toe of the corpse. This same ring, placed on the finger of a living person, made him or her appear dead until it was removed.

Today, the term "living dead" conjures up an image of zombies created by voodoo magic. So what's the truth behind zombies? Haitian law contains a big clue. It's illegal in Haiti to give anyone a substance that makes them fall into a coma so they can be buried as dead. Some believe that an old voodoo practice persists to this day—a sorcerer, or bokor, drugs a victim so that he remains conscious yet cannot speak or move. To all outward appearances, he's dead. So, he's buried, only to be dug up again within 72 hours as a zombie, the walking-dead slave to the bokor.

Powerful Mind Games

Hawaii has a history of magical folk religion that's similar to voodoo. Sorcerers known as *kahuna ana'anas* had the power to kill someone by eating a stew containing something taken from the victim and by saying a death prayer. The next day the sorcerer would tell the victim he was cursed to die and that the first sign would be a tingling sensation in the feet. Most people have pins and needles from time to time, so you can imagine the fear caused by the slightest tingle. Eventually, constant fear, lack of sleep and loss of appetite would take such a toll on the health of the victim that he would give up and die. If you think this sounds far-fetched, it's not. We now know, for instance, that constant stress can disarm the immune system, preventing infections and wounds from healing.

How Charming...

Not all voodoo magic is harmful. Some of its talismans and amulets are intended to attract friendly spirits. Love dolls are supposed to bind someone's love to you. Charm lamps—containing sugar, honey, perfume, flower petals and bits of sheep's brain—are also meant to attract the love of a particular person.

Toadskin and Fish Livers

No, it's not a recipe for soup. Haitian sorcerors, called bokors, drug their victims with poison from the skin of a toad and ground-up puffer fish. The toad poison causes hallucinations. Tetrodotoxin, the poison found in the liver of puffer fish (shown below), is so strong just the tiniest amount causes total paralysis. It slows the heartbeat and causes such shallow breathing that they're difficult to detect.

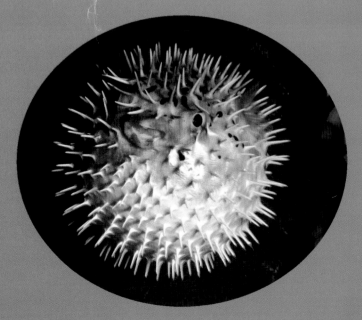

Which witch is which?

Witchcraft

She's ugly, old and warty, and flies a state-of-the-art broomstick. That's the popular Halloween image of the witch. It's most likely a warped version of the crone, a wise old goddess of an ancient religion called Wicca (pronounced "witcha").

For thousands of years, if disease struck your family, your livestock or your crops, people blamed it on witchcraft. No one knew about viruses or bacteria that could attack plants and animals. Putting witches to death came to a head with the witch hunts of Europe. For 200 years no one was safe—but if you were a woman living alone with a cat, and knew anything about plants, you might as well put out a sign saying "Witch lives here." It was especially dangerous to make enemies. A farmer whose cow suddenly stopped giving milk could easily accuse a disliked neighbor of putting the evil eye on the cow. She'd be arrested and tortured until she "confessed." Then she'd either be burned at the stake or hanged.

Witch-hunting continued as Europeans moved to the United States. In 1692, several girls in Salem, Massachusetts, began to suffer convulsions and hallucinations; they shrieked during prayers, made wild gestures and talked gibberish. They said they felt as if they were being pinched and bitten. Witchcraft was suspected and, by the time the investigation was over, 150 people were accused of bewitching the girls—95 were executed.

By the late 20th century, a psychologist wondered if there was a natural cause for the girls' symptoms. She discovered that people who eat a fungus called ergot suffer from convulsions and hallucinations. Ergot sometimes poisons rye grown on moist, shaded land, like that around Salem. Outbreaks of ergot poisoning in Europe throughout the Middle Ages were often followed by witchcraft persecutions.

KITCHEN WITCHES

A kitchen, or cottage, witch is a "good" witch, skilled in all kinds of home-based magic. Match up each object with its correct action to see how knowledgeable a kitchen witch you would make. (Answers on page 40.)

1. **A jar containing three needles, three pins, three nails and salt.**
2. **An onion on the windowsill.**
3. **Copper moulds on the wall.**
4. **Two brooms.**
5. **Many sieves and colanders.**

a. **Crossed on the wall, these are a protective sign.**
b. **Guards the kitchen from harm.**
c. **Their holes sift out negative energies.**
d. **A Witch's Bottle in a cupboard helps prevent food contamination (especially if you keep everything clean!).**
e. **These bring the power of Venus to the kitchen, making it a loving place.**

Magic Root

What's shaped like a tiny human body and supposedly shrieks when you pull it out of the ground? It's a mandrake root. Legend says that to hear its screams is lethal, so you have to cover your ears before tricking a dog into uprooting the plant. For centuries midwives used mandrake to calm women who were going through a difficult childbirth. The plant's ability to change behavior and its human-like form helped fuel the belief that midwives who used it must be witches. Today we know that mandrake contains the powerful drug, scopolamine, renowned for its soothing effect on people who are anxious or upset.

The Magic
ARTS

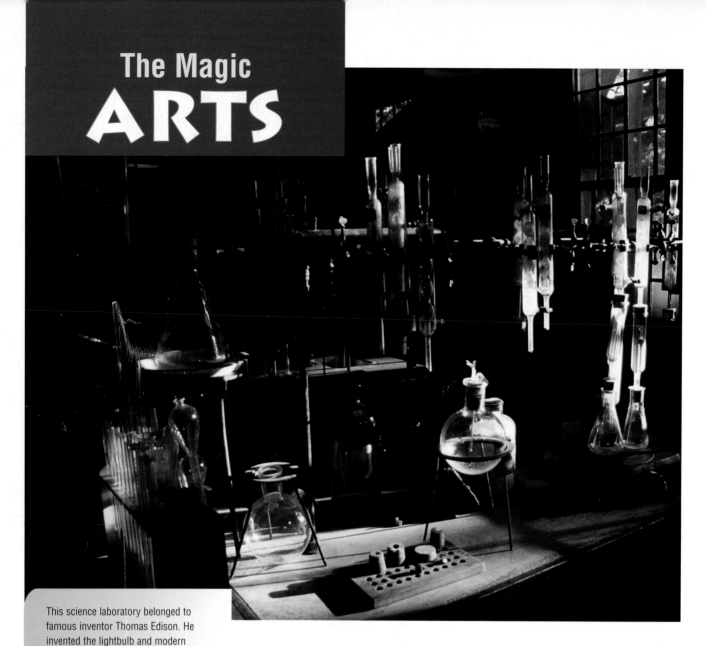

This science laboratory belonged to famous inventor Thomas Edison. He invented the lightbulb and modern sound recording among glass beakers and tubes, and using burners and racks just like the ones used by alchemists for hundreds of years.

Step into my laboratory...

Alchemy

In the past, science and magic were the same thing. Alchemists were magicians whose driving ambition was to find the philosopher's stone. This elusive substance supposedly had the power to transform base metal like lead into gold or silver, and it was thought to prolong life. But being a wizard at chemistry wasn't enough to guarantee success. You had to know your astrology too. It was believed that, to create the purest form of silver, you had to work under a waxing moon.

Alchemists put in long hours over hot furnaces. They believed an ancient Greek idea that all matter can be reduced down to four elements: earth, air, fire and water. If all metals are composed of these four elements in varying proportions, why not take common metals and recombine the elements to create more precious forms of matter, like gold and silver?

I'm Not Dead Yet!

Scientists have been searching for a modern day equivalent to the philosopher's stone that will help us all live longer. They think they might have found it in one of the genes of a fruit fly, shown at right. They named the gene "I'm not dead yet", or Indy for short. By altering this gene so that fruit flies use and store energy differently, scientists have increased their lifespan from the normal 37 days to as long as 71 days.

A Wizard's Warning

A long time ago someone named Albert the Great wrote a how-to book on alchemy in which he recommends setting up a laboratory in a secluded location so as not to upset the neighbors in case things go wrong. And experiments do go wrong, as an unfortunate rocket scientist from the California Institute of Technology demonstrated in June 1952. Apparently, he was attempting to reconstruct an alchemical experiment from the Middle Ages when he blew himself and his garage laboratory to pieces.

Too bad alchemists didn't base their work on an even older Greek idea that the universe is made out of tiny particles called atoms—an idea that is correct! Today we know that an element is any substance that is made up entirely of one kind of atom. So you can't combine anything to form an element. Gold and silver are both elements. But elements are rarely found on their own in nature. Most of the substances you can see around you, such as water, are compounds, formed when two or more elements bond together during a chemical reaction.

But, even though their ideas weren't always right, alchemists didn't entirely waste their time. They developed sophisticated chemical equipment, like the crucibles used to heat up and purify substances. And they discovered chemical dyes.

Tools of the TRADE

Drums and Rattles

The hypnotic beat of the drum and shaking of the rattle help the shaman achieve a trance-like state of consciousness, during which he or she can journey into the world of spirits. If the repeated shaking of a rattle can eventually bring on a dream-like state, do you suppose this is why it's one of the first toys we give to babies?

Broomsticks

Modern witches use a broom, or besom, to sweep an area clean of unwanted energies, but witches of long ago used to fly on them. Or so they thought. They probably took a drug that gave them the sensation of leaving the ground. One such drug comes from a highly poisonous mushroom. The only safe way to take it is to drink the urine of the unfortunate victim who has eaten it. Why? Because its harmful chemicals are broken down in the victim's liver, while the safer ones that cause the sensation of flight pass unaltered into the urine.

Magical Charms

Belief in the magical power of objects is found all over the world. Amulets, like the magic square shown here (the numbers in a row in any direction add up to 34!), protect the wearer from the evil eye. Talismans—pieces of stone, metal, glass or wood inscribed with words and symbols—bring good luck and protect from harm. Maybe the real magic is in the way the wearers make their own good luck, with these things as constant reminders to keep trying.

Wands

Magicians use wands to conduct and generate magical energy. A wand might be a simple stick or elaborately decorated with a stone or crystal at the tip. It gives the magician an air of authority and helps focus attention and energies on the task at hand. Think of a conductor trying to conduct an orchestra without a wand, or baton.

Magic Circle

Calling up evil spirits held risks for magicians wanting to cast evil spells. To protect themselves, they stood inside a circle drawn in the earth with a sword or knife. The circle also represented a sphere, a miniature version of the universe. By directing events inside the circle, magicians believed they could direct events in the world at large.

Presto! Change-o!

Stage Magic

Stage magicians are masters of illusion. They make sure that you see only what they want you to see, not what's really going on. It helps that we only take in a small amount of visual information at a time, and this can make us blind to changes.

Two American psychologists tested this idea. Imagine you're walking along and a woman asks you for directions. Your conversation is interrupted when two men, carrying an upright wooden door, walk between you. The woman says that you've just taken part in a psychology experiment and asks if you noticed anything change after the men passed by. If you say, "No," you feel like a real fool when she tells you that she's not the same woman who asked you for directions! The door was

used like a magician's prop, allowing a different woman to walk up behind it and change places with the one you were talking to, who walked off.

Unbelievably, half of all people tested were victims of "change blindness"—they didn't realize they'd been talking to two different people! It happens because we don't store elaborate scenes in our short-term memory. Instead, we note what has changed and assume the rest has remained the same. If we miss the change, we are liable to think everything is the same.

LOOK AGAIN

Do you remember seeing this illustration a few pages ago? Has anything changed? Go back to page 29 and see if you can spot the difference. (Answer on page 40.)

Misdirection

A magician can make a coin seem to vanish by hiding it in her right hand while pretending she placed it in her left. How can your brain be tricked so easily? If she simply opened her left hand to show it's empty, you'd immediately look at her right hand because that's where you last saw the coin. So she misdirects you by looking and pointing at her left hand, knowing that you'll look where she looks. And she'll keep the misdirection going by rubbing or blowing on her left hand. The more she builds up the misdirection, the greater the illusion she creates that the coin really did vanish.

Blue Magic

Ever since the Chinese developed gunpowder more than 1000 years ago, magicians have used it for special effects. But ancient fireworks were nowhere near as spectacular or colorful as they are today. Modern firework manufacturers can produce gold sparks, intense white or yellow-orange light, even red and green. But blue is a challenge. The best blue comes from copper chloride, but it's unstable at the high temperatures needed to produce intense light. So if you see a fireworks display with vivid blues in it, be impressed—whoever created the fireworks is a chemical wizard.

In his 1902 film *A Trip to the Moon*, Georges Méliès helped invent the screen magic of special effects.

Hocus pocus
. . . focus!

Screen Magic

"Moving pictures" were invented about 100 years ago and a French magician named Georges Méliès soon became a pioneer of magical special effects. One of his short films shows a tiny dancer performing on a table, as if by magic. The audience was astounded. How did he do it? Méliès filmed the table close up, rewound the film and used it again to film the dancer from farther away. When he shot the table, he used a matte to block out the small area where the dancer would appear—when he filmed the dancer, he matted out the surroundings.

Today, early special effects in movies look funny to us because we're used to the fantastic special effects that can be created by the digital technology of computers. Think back on some of your favorite movies over the past few years. Did any of the characters morph into another shape, walk up walls or generally do something that ordinary people could never do? Well, they didn't really do it—but you knew that, didn't you?

Digital technology is one of the latest magic tools in the world of film make-believe and, like necromancers of old, it can even appear to bring people back to life. If an actor dies before filming is completed, skilled production technologists can use digital processes to recreate his moving image from previously shot film and insert it into scenes that he hadn't been able to complete. Some people even predict that, one day, living actors might no longer be needed. How would you feel about going to the movies to see a star who never existed outside of a computer screen?

What's Up Doc?

Things happen in the zany world of cartoons that could never happen in real life. For instance, how many cartoon characters have you seen squashed completely flat only to bounce back to their normal shape? In the quirky world of quantum physics, when soliton waves collide and get squashed out of shape, they act just like cartoon characters and bounce back to their normal shape again.

The Magic Box

Remember the replicator on Star Trek's *Enterprise*? Using a technology like magic, it could make anything the crew requested. Researchers have created a 3-D printer they hope one day will rival any science-fiction technology. A regular printer lays down a single layer of ink on a sheet of paper, but a 3-D printer deposits layer upon layer of plastic, metal, paper or acrylic until it builds a three-dimensional object. The United States Army plans to use a truck-mounted 3-D printer to create instant replacement parts for any vehicle that breaks down. In future, if your favorite toy or piece of equipment breaks down, all you'll have to do is download a program from the Internet and 3-D print a new one.

Magic TODAY

13

SPOT THE SUPERSTITION

How many people in the picture above are acting on their superstitions? Where do you think these beliefs came from? Look for the answers on page 40.

Believe in Magic

Back in the 1980s a professor at the University of Pennsylvania conducted an unusual experiment. He presented his students, one at a time, with two empty boxes and two labels. One label read "sugar" and the other "sodium cyanide," which is a poison. The professor poured sugar into both boxes and asked the students to stick a label on each box. Then he asked them to taste the sugar. Most didn't want to taste the sugar in the box marked cyanide, even though they knew it was sugar. Why?

Very young children go through a stage of magical thinking when they confuse the name of an object with the actual object. Could these university students have reverted back to the magical thinking of childhood and suddenly become afraid of a box of sugar, just because of the name they'd given it?

If you asked any of these students if they believed in magic, they'd probably deny it. But if they're superstitious, they believe in a form of magic. And surveys have shown that college students all over North America can be very superstitious. They go into exams wearing lucky clothes or a lucky charm, making sure they have their lucky pen that helped them do well on the last exam.

Who's Superstitious?

Professional athletes are put under stress to perform well in front of an audience, and they can be extremely superstitious. Many develop rituals that help block anxiety and slow the pulse and breathing. A ritual becomes truly superstitious when the performer believes that it can affect what's going to happen next. The baseball player who never washes his socks during a winning streak, or wears his hat backwards to reverse a losing streak, is firmly in the grip of magic. Hockey star Wayne Gretzky, at right, always tucked the right side of his jersey behind his hip pads, a superstition that lots of players have copied in hopes of playing like The Great One.

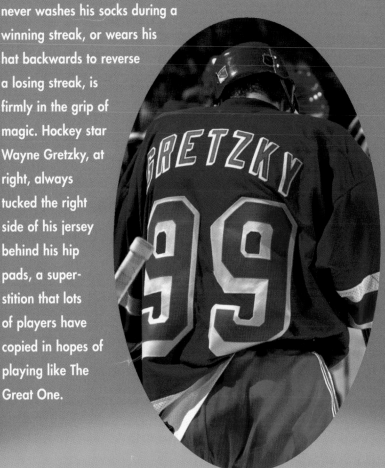

Clowning Around

In 1987, two American researchers conducted an experiment by placing very young children in a room so they could watch the children without being seen. A child-sized mechanical clown named Bobo dispensed marbles from his mouth on a set schedule. Thinking that the marbles appeared because of what they were doing, three quarters of the children developed a superstitious ritual based on what they were doing when Bobo produced a marble. These rituals included wiggling hips, kissing the clown, touching his face in a certain way and smiling or grimacing at him.

In many parts of the world, science and technology have taken the place of magic. Scientists research long hours and work as hard as any alchemist. But today, instead of the philosopher's stone, scientists are trying to achieve a process that seems almost magical. It's called "cold fusion," and would offer a way to harness the power of nuclear fusion—the process that powers the sun—using water at room temperature. If scientists could pull this off, they could provide the world with cheap, abundant, pollution-free energy. In 1989, two chemists in the U.S. thought they succeeded in achieving cold fusion in a test tube—but they didn't. Cold fusion remains as elusive to today's scientists as the philosopher's stone was to alchemists long ago.

Many of us might look to modern science instead of magic to explain things we don't understand, but we can't seem to give up on our magical beliefs. In the same way, even though psychologists explain reasons for the magical thinking we go through in childhood, most of us want to hold on to some of that thinking even when we grow up. Who knows why we persist in wanting to believe in magic? Could it be that magic has been around for thousands of years, while the modern version of science is new in comparison? If that's the case, it's going to take a long time for magic to disappear entirely from our lives. So relax and enjoy it while it lasts.

Wave a Magic Wand

In the future, surgeons and designers will be able to turn a flat image on a computer screen into a 3-D image that floats in mid-air. If the 3-D image is of a brain scan, a surgeon can turn it around, with the wave of a wand, to locate an injury. And a car designer can use the wand to change the shape of a car and see instantly what it would look like. The magic behind this technology is a ferro-liquid crystal screen that projects the image into the air. What 3-D image would you create with your magic wand?

Look into the Magic Crystal

Scientists looking for mysterious dark matter in space think it might contain lots of Weakly Interacting Massive Particles, or WIMPs for short. They suspended a large crystal of sodium iodide inside a vat of water at the bottom of a mine. After five years, the crystal started to flash, as WIMP after WIMP passed through it. If space contains enough WIMPs, the combined pull of their gravity will eventually stop the universe expanding. It will then contract and—in several billion years—the universe will end in a big crunch. How's that for telling the future in a magic crystal?

ANSWERS

Just a Job, page 9
Doctors and midwives prescribed herbs, which were thought to contain the magical powers of nature. Blacksmiths knew the secrets of metals, which were also thought to have magical properties. Barbers cut hair, which could be used in spells. Shepherds spent their lives outdoors, close to the magical forces of nature. And gravediggers spent so much time with the dead, they must surely know some of their secrets.

It's All About You, page 21
You'll probably find that systems of foretelling the future—such as the runes on page 18, Tarot cards, palm reading, the I Ching or astrology—always seem to give you a message that relates to your situation. Uncanny, isn't it? That's because they never give specific answers to specific questions. They never tell you, for instance, to stay home and study for your math exam instead of going to the movies. Instead, you might turn up an answer that says, "Recognize what you need to reach your goal." You can interpret this any way you wish. But if you're wise, you'll interpret it to mean, "If you stay home tonight and study, you'll pass your math exam."

Kitchen Witches, page 27
1,d; 2, b; 3, e; 4, a; 5, c.

Look Again, page 33
On page 29, the scientist shown is a man; on page 33, the scientist has changed to a woman!

Spot the Superstition, page 36
There are a total of 7 different examples of superstition in this picture.

1. Breaking a mirror is bad luck because of the belief that a person's reflection contains his or her soul. The Romans who set the bad luck at seven years were on the right track: your bones renew themselves completely every seven years.

2. Walking under a ladder is thought to be bad luck. Leaning against the wall, ladders form a triangle, the sacred symbol of life. Walking through a triangle was thought to put your life in danger.

3. Placing a horseshoe above or near a doorway is thought to bring protection and good fortune to the family living in the house. If the open end points up, good luck can accumulate in the shoe's opening; if the horseshoe points down, the good luck it brings can be showered on whoever walks under it. Which way do you prefer your lucky horseshoe?

4. Fear of the number thirteen might go back to a Norse legend in which a god crashed a feast given for 12 gods (he brought the guest list up to 13). Trouble broke out, and the uninvited thirteenth guest caused the death of everyone's favorite god!

5. A black cat is probably the world's most famous bad luck symbol—except in Britain, where it's supposed to be lucky. Why is it bad luck? It's probably its color—the color of night and the powers of darkness.

6. Standing under an umbrella indoors is believed to bring bad luck to everyone living in the building. Originally, African royalty used umbrellas to shield themselves from the hot rays of the sun, which was seen as a god. Opening an umbrella indoors insulted the sun god, an action that would make the god take punishment on the offender.

7. Tying a string around your finger is popularly thought to help you remember something. It also follows an ancient belief that a knot was a charm against evil. If a demon saw the knot, it would become intrigued by the knot's complex shape and forget about bothering you.